Kintsugi Your Heart

The Art Of Living With Grief

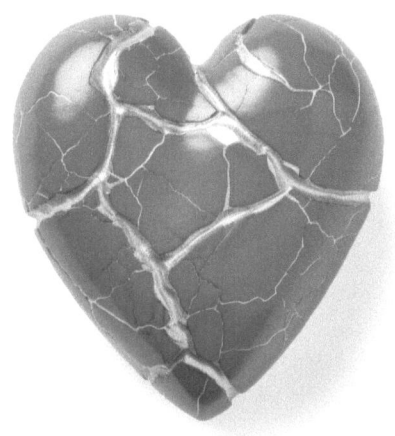

Carol Banens

Carol Banens
Copyright © 2023

All rights reserved. No part of this book may be reproduced, stored
in a retrieval system, or transmitted in any form or by any means,
electronic, mechanical, photocopying, recording, scanning,
or otherwise, without the prior written consent of the author.

Dedication

*To my late husband, Brian Browne,
jazz pianist extraordinaire.
Forever in my heart.*

Contents

Introduction	7
Shattered	**9**
Free To Go	10
A Peaceful Exit	11
The Grief Of Loss	12
I Thought I Was Prepared	13
The Solitude Of Grief	15
There's Just So Much Time	16
Now That they've Gone	16
Stop Fighting Me!	17
Some Days…	19
Losing You, Losing Me	20
How Are You?	22
The Invisible Cloak Of Grief	23
Grief May Be Postponed, But Not Erased	24
My Stranded Soul	26
You're Doing So Well!	27
Flattened By Grief	29
Walking Through The Mist	30
Taking Refuge	31
If My Heart Could Speak	33
Permission To Grieve	34
Rivers Of Sadness	36
A Soul Locked Down	37
Fermenting Grief	39
In Pieces	**43**
The Last Act Of love	44
Life Marches On	45
Not Dealing Is Not Dealing!	46
I see you	48

Your Presence Surrounds Me	49
I Cried Out For You	50
I Played For You	51
The Anniversary	52
The Space Between Us	53
Embracing Life	54
Transforming Your Relationship	55
Bearing Witness	57
Holding Back	58
Triggered	59
Avalanche	60
Aimless	61
Spirit to Spirit	62
Growing Through Grief	63
Embracing Pain, Maintaining Hope	64

Making Broken Beautiful	**67**
By The Thickness Of A Sheet Of Paper!	68
Transcend	69
Running Toward Life Not Away	70
Tethered	71
Discovering You	72
Courage Revealed	74
The Waves Of Grief Still Come	75
Avenue To Your Healing	76
Crossing The Threshold,	77
The Power Of Hope	79
The Mosaic Of Life	81
Illuminating The Colours	82
Of Life After Grief	82
Kintsugi Your Heart With Love	83
The Grief Remains, But You Expand Around It	85

A Brighter Tomorrow	87
Dear Grief…	88
The Choice You Make	90
Don't Stop Living Because I Died	91
Opening To Possibilities As You Move Through Grief	92
A New Life Unfolding	94
The Woman I've Become	95
Cracked Open	97
Acknowledgements	99
What Others Have Said About Working With Carol	101
Also by Carol Banens	102
About the Author	103
A Note from the Author	104
Free Resources to Support You On Your Grief Journey	105

Introduction

Dear Griever, Carer of a Griever, or Reader,

The grief journey is a hard one to take, and I want to help guide you from your shattered heart, through picking up the pieces, to a place where they are finally 'kintsugi'd' together again.

The Japanese art of Kintsugi is where a broken pot is put back together with gold, making something beautiful, but different from the original.

This to me is what happens in grief. Our hearts are shattered and then we have to put the pieces back together... in the end coming back to life, but a different one, and with the possibility of it still being beautiful, despite our loss.

The poems are divided into three sections.
Shattered
In Pieces
Making Broken Beautiful

Each grief journey is unique, and these poems reflect my journey whilst still touching on universal themes.

It is my hope that by laying open the painful emotions of grief, especially the ones that society doesn't talk about, you'll be able to see you are not alone with them.

So whether you're the griever or there is someone you know who is grieving, I hope this gives you a way to connect and move through your grief to a place where you can begin to embrace life again.

With love and gratitude,
Carol

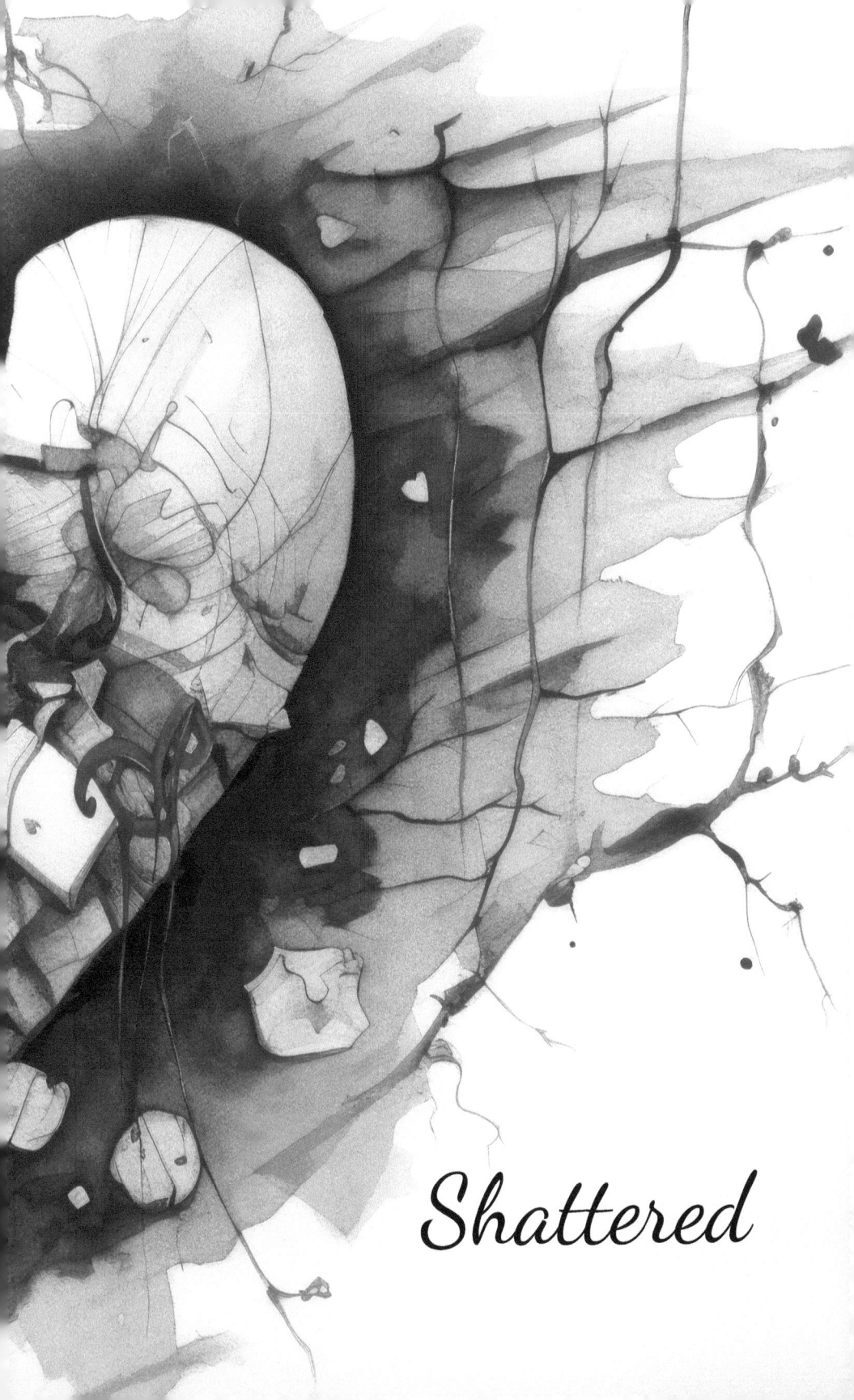

Free To Go

I let go of your hand
Just for a moment,
And in that split second
You left me

No longer tethered to me...
With my hand softly in yours
Holding on
For dear life,
Your life,
You were free to go

Forgive me my love,
I couldn't stay there with you
For it was no longer you.
The pain of seeing you, but not you
Was too much

I left the room
No sitting beside you for a while
No talking to you
I fled

Your last days
Were filled with my love.
Hands held except for that last moment,
Physically, you were gone
But spiritually, ever present.

✦

A Peaceful Exit

How you dreaded
Not being able to breathe,
To be gasping.
But it was not so, my love,
We made sure of that.

As I transferred you into the bed one last time
I held you in my arms
As if it were one last dance
Knowing that there would be no other hugs
This was it.

And I lay in a bed next to you
For four days and nights
I held your hand
Talking to you,
As you drifted into a deeper and deeper sleep.

Your breath was calm
It was not laboured
It was shallow, soft
Easy

Your transition to the other realm
Was exactly the peaceful exit you wanted.

✦

The Grief Of Loss

You can't imagine it
Until you are in it,
The painful loss of a loved one

You wake
Hoping it isn't true
And then realise it is
And curl up under the covers
Wishing that sleep would take you away for just a little longer

But no... it has to be faced
To be processed
To be journeyed through

Loving greatly
Means grieving deeply
Shattered heart
Mind distracted
Everything just feels wrong

But out of loss
Can we find some strength
To allow us to grow alongside the grief
Rather than be defined by it?
I think so

When you tend to your heart
With love and understanding
The healing can begin.

✦

I Thought I Was Prepared

We knew it was coming
Cancer can do that
Give you a glimpse
Of the future

You were so amazing, my love,
Never complaining
Music keeping you healthy
For so much longer than expected

And I thought I was prepared
Everything was organised
Funeral, music, readings, obituary…
But I wasn't

How could I be?
I'd never lost a husband before

The depth of pain
Overwhelmed me
I was shocked
Almost catatonic
No, I wasn't prepared

Body heavy with grief
Mind completely fogged,
Heart aching with pain.
This, this was not what I'd expected
Not this hard, not this deep, not this long
Just not this

As I look back,
I see that you can't really prepare
For the emotional turmoil
That upends your life
When the love of your life
Dies.

✦

The Solitude Of Grief

In the aftermath of the funeral
Life becomes quieter,
The visitors mainly drop off
And you are left,
Surrounded by a deafening silence

The hush of the house,
The emptiness,
It envelops you
And you feel quite alone

Grief can feel lonely
The lack of understanding
The 'no one knows how I'm feeling'
Can feel isolating

And so you retreat into solitude
Sitting with your thoughts, your pain
Trying to make sense of this new situation

Perhaps the solitude
Is one of the paths to healing
Allowing you to listen and feel
What you'd rather not,
But need to.

There's Just So Much Time Now That they've Gone

As a caregiver to your loved one
Your day was full
Appointments to the hospital
Professionals visiting the house

But after your loved one is gone
You all of a sudden have time
So expansive
That you are lost

The silence surrounding you
The not knowing what to do next
Leaves you floundering
With nothing to do

And then the isolation
Can lead to depression
And where you were once needed
It feels as though
Your meaning has been stripped from you
And you sit with…

'What Now…?'

✦

Stop Fighting Me!

Hello dear one,
I'm your grief
And I want to be heard,
To be listened to

Oh I know you'd rather not,
That's why you distract yourself
Keep busy
Drink a little more than usual
Anything but tune into me

But I have something to say
It is normal for you to hurt like this
When you've loved, you'll grieve
I want you to feel the pain of loss,
To experience the absence,
To explore memories,
I want, in fact
To be your companion for life

You see, I'm here now,
I can't be pushed down, or pushed away
I can't be ignored, or postponed
I am now a part of you,
A friend of sorts
That travels each day,
Just in the background
But there nevertheless

So dear one,
Stop fighting me...
Allow me to be with you
Acknowledge my presence,
Know that I'll soften over time
And that every now and then,
I'll just whisper to you
To remind you that I'm here.

Some Days...

Some days
You'd prefer to stay in bed,
Pull the covers over you,
Feel the weight of the blankets
Somehow comforting the heaviness of your grief

You curl up
Eyes squeezed tightly shut,
Let it not be true
Not be real
Let me come out of my cocoon
To find you here
Beside me

But you know
As you hide in your tented covers,
That today is one of those days,
A day pregnant with grief from the moment you wake
Til the moment you try to sleep

So dear one,
Be kind to yourself,
Rest a little
Sleep a little
Cry a little
Or cry a lot

For although you won't believe me if I tell you,
This too shall pass
Someday
One day.

✦

Losing You, Losing Me

You were lost.
Gone.
And me?
It turns out I'd lost me too.

Without you
Without us
I was not me anymore
That me?
She died right beside you

But who was I now?
That was the question
What brought me joy?
I didn't know
What did I love?
I didn't know
What did I want?
I didn't know

Oh my love, I didn't just lose you
Lose your music
Lose your smile
Lose your jokes,
I lost me too.

And that was unexpected,
At the worst time of my life
Suddenly
I didn't have a clue who I was anymore

Losing you, losing me
A grief doubled.

✦

How Are You?

'How are you?' they say
How do you think?

I'm dying inside
Heart breaking
I feel leaden
Crushed by the weight of grief

My body aches
Fatigue overwhelming me
Brain out of sync
Not knowing if it is coming or going

I am lost
Utterly and completely bereft
I can't imagine life without him
Without my love

The anguish of his absence
Consumes every moment
Each breath, heavy with sorrow

How am I?
I'll probably tell you I'm fine
But know this…
I'm dying inside.

✦

The Invisible Cloak Of Grief

It's wrapped around you
This invisible cloak,
No one can see it
It's texture
It's colours of grey and black

But it is there
Constricting your breath
Squeezing the life out of you

You feel it
Reaching into your heart
Silently suffocating your joy

But no one understands
The weight of this cloak
Until the day they lose a loved one
And it lands on their shoulders
Quietly burdening them
With sorrow.

✦

Grief May Be Postponed, But Not Erased

Sometimes it feels too much,
The emotional rollercoaster
Affecting every moment, no, every second of your day.
You just can't focus
Nothing feels right

And it isn't
Your loved one is gone
You are trying to navigate through tidal waves of grief
And you think...
What if I just push it down?

You shut it away in a box,
Put it on a shelf
In the dark recess of your mind
And plan to deal with it later
When you feel better

If only we could do that,
But postponing grief, doesn't make it go away
It waits, lurking in the darkness
For the exact moment to catch you off guard.

You've used so much energy
Keeping it at bay,
You thought you were in control.
But not so,
It cries out for you to pay it attention
It needs to be heard and felt

I remember as I did just this
Avoiding it
Trying to delay it
It came back, only to totally overwhelm me
Stopping me in my tracks

And all it was doing,
Was crying out for my attention.

My Stranded Soul

Without you
My world is no longer the same
Heart shattered
Soul stranded
In a sea of grief

Let there be
An invisible tether
Connecting us
Silently conveying love,
Still

Without you
I am lost
Empty
Peace eludes me
My soul stranded
A hostage to grief.

✦

You're Doing So Well!

Ahh but I'm not.
Do you mean that I'm a quiet griever
That I shield you from my tears
From the uncomfortableness
Of it all?

Do you mean that I am keeping it together
That I look fine
That I don't talk about it
That I'm back to normal?
I'm not

Do you mean I'm strong
Not showing any emotion
Appearing to be coping just fine
I'm not

You see...
Grief is not supposed to be done in silence
In the shadow of your home.
It is not meant to be done behind a veil
Where you can't express your sorrow

Am I doing well?
No.
I just know
That others can't cope
If I mourn openly
Shed tears
Break down

For grief is still taboo

And so I go home
And there I collapse
The burden of a facade
Finally allowed to let go.

✦

Flattened By Grief

I sit here
Joyless
Empty
Engulfed in my grief

I push away the feelings of sadness
Down I shove them
Compressed inside

But with them go
Other emotions
Joy, happiness, contentment

And so here I am
Avoiding my pain
But also suppressing
All my other emotions

It is time, dear one,
To decompress
Allow the pain to bubble up
Feel it, cry tears of sorrow

And perhaps,
As the pain softens
You'll notice
That you are able to smile
Once more.

✦

Walking Through The Mist

Everything is foggy
Clarity has disappeared
The path is not clear
Where should I go?

There is a cloud of mist
At every step
Engulfing me in pain
Blocking my way

Is there life ahead
But hidden?
Is there a doorway
For me to pass through

Shine a light
Guide me
Show me the way
For now
I'm lost,
Blinded by the mist
Of tears and sorrow.

Taking Refuge

Where can I go to escape this pain?
You can't, it must be faced
But it is too much
Unbearable
No, it is bearable, you'll see

Dear one,
Take refuge in your heart
For that is where love resides
Take refuge in the stillness
And breathe

Breathe in and out
Into your heartspace
Lovingly tending
To your pain
Breathe care into your being
As you take refuge
In the peace of your soul.

Sit with the pain my love
Hard as it is.
Just for a moment
Allow it, breathe it
And know that retreating
Inside
Will let your pain have a voice
It will be heard
Felt
And as such
Ever so gently soften

Take refuge dear one
In your heart of hearts.

✦

→ *If you'd like the free meditation that goes along with this poem, go to the back page and scan the QR code.*

If My Heart Could Speak

If my heart could speak
It would shout out
Come back to me my love
I can't go on without you

If my heart could speak
It would whisper
I love you
I love you

If my heart could speak
It might break as the words
Tumbled out like
Falling rocks

If my heart could speak
It would ask to be healed
To be held together
By your love

If my heart could speak
It would say
Here, here you may stay
As cherished memories
Tucked away
Surrounded by the beating pulse of love
That is my heart.

✦

Permission To Grieve

You are so busy
You have work to do
People to care for
Arrangements to make

You have no time
To mourn
You shelve it
Push it away
Thinking that is what you should do

But, dear one,
Did anyone tell you
You have permission to grieve?

You are allowed to slow down
To rest
To say no
To cry
To take time

Your grief needs to be attended to
You don't need anyone's permission.
So you may have to be the one
Who speaks up,
Who prioritises self-care,
Who learns how to self-nurture

Don't wait for permission.
You won't get it from anyone other than yourself...
Except for me.
They don't realise
The needs you have,
The requirements
To move yourself
Onward through this journey of loss

If you look ok,
If you act ok
You must be ok!

Feel the grief
Mourn outwardly
Give yourself the permission you need
To start healing.

✦

Rivers Of Sadness

The tears kept flowing
Rivers of sadness
Drowning my cheeks

You were gone,
I knew it was happening
It was expected,
But the depth of sorrow
Brought me to my knees

The teary droplets
Gushed like a raging river
Trying to rid myself
Of the pain,
Wash it away
Cleanse my heart

And they didn't stop
A constant flow of grief
Expressing my love
In the only way possible
In that moment

Rivers of sadness
Engulfed my being
As I allowed
The immensity of loss
To be released.

✦

A Soul Locked Down

Your soulmate... gone
And your own soul
Locked down in grief

The shadow of loss
Envelops you
Cloaked in black
Head hung low
Life constricted

What can be done
To free yourself
Your soul?

It is love, of course
Self-compassion, kindness
These are the keys
To breaking open
The hard shell
Restricting your soul

Let love in
Tenderly, freely
And feel how it softens
And splits apart
The chains of grief

Allow
Accept
And release
Your soul
To experience what love is
Once more.

Fermenting Grief

The temptation when in so much pain
Is to push it down
Ignore
Distract
Try and relegate it to a dark corner

But there it will sit,
Grief fermenting,
Bubbling away
Beneath the surface of your life,
Seeping into your cells
One by one

Until the lid can't be kept on it any longer
It is released with such force
That you don't know what hit you

It was the grief you'd tucked away
To deal with later
But now grown,
Expanded,
Stronger

The answer, dear one
Is not to resist
These painful feelings
But to do what seems perplexing,
And that is
To allow

Resisting leads to persisting,
A burgeoning grief.
Allowing, surprisingly,
Lets it soften
Losing strength
Until it becomes
Bearable.

✦

Carol Danens

In Pieces

The Last Act Of love

Is this grief
Really the last act of love?
Is my broken heart
In fact a loving heart
Just weeping for your absence?

Oh my love
I don't think so,
For grieving may soften
It may even be hidden for most of the time
But my love for you?
Never ending

Grieving you
Is one way of expressing my love
But not the last act
No…

For loving you does not stop because you are not there
Loving you continues
Over a lifetime
Until I join you
In my last breath.

✦

Life Marches On

'Don't they all know?
I'm mourning my loved one'
'No my love, most do not'

As you sit
Shattered, Overwhelmed, Exhausted
Unsure what the next step is,
Life marches on around you

Nothing stops for your grief
The days blend into night
The sun rises and falls
The stars still shine above
And yet for you...
It is as if everything has come to a grinding halt

And it is ok, for you to stop
To feel, to cry, to rest
Because although everything else goes on as normal,
Nothing now is normal for you

Take refuge, dear one,
From the busyness of the world,
Create a space where for you, time stands still
Just for a while,
And give yourself
Permission
To mourn fully.

✦

Not Dealing Is Not Dealing!

Burying your head under the covers
You just want to disappear
The warmth and safety you feel
Comforts you momentarily

And you decide
You're not even getting up
Not today, and maybe not tomorrow
You'll just pretend
Like this,
This loss
Didn't happen

But how long
Can you keep that up
Dealing with grief
By not dealing?

It just doesn't work that way
I know dear one,
If only it did

But hibernating doesn't truly ease it
Not for the long haul.

So let me encourage you
Hard as it may be
To poke your head out of your cave
And allow just a little grief in

Not too much
Not the whole shebang
Just a morsel
Small enough that you can bear it

And then each day
As you add just a little more
You'll find
That dealing with your grief
Is actually the way through it.

✦

I see you

I'm here my love
Watching you mourn
Your grief consuming you

If only I could let you know
I'm in bliss
Words cannot describe the beauty of being free
Free of the pain

My essence in the ether
Surrounds you
Trying to comfort you
When you cry

My love, don't cry
I am at peace
But you?
I see you,
The turmoil
The sadness

It is time, to move through
This awful grief you feel
Allow yourself grace
I am always with you
And...
I see you

✦

Your Presence Surrounds Me

It's not the things that I see
It is the you that I sense
Still here, keeping an eye on me

I imagine what you'd say to me
And smile
Knowing how irreverent you always were
Now, I can chuckle at those thoughts

And when I'm at the piano
I sense your presence,
Guiding me to the right chords
Channelling the very sound of you
Allowing me to keep my connection with you

Surround me with your presence my love
It comforts me to know.

✦

I Cried Out For You

Oh my love
Where are you?
Show me a sign, please
Let me know you are with me

Send me a Blue Jay
Let one be a signal that you are watching over me...
With me still

And with that I closed my teary eyes to meditate
Slowing my breath
I gently relaxed
And then
Opening my eyes
What should I see
But two Blue Jays sitting on the deck, looking right back at me.

Thank you my love
So nice to see you

✦

I Played For You

I sat at the piano
Tears streaming down my face
How could I play
When you were no longer there?

Oh my love
How I miss your music
I heard you tell me
'Play some Blues Babe'
And with that, in that very moment
I smelled your aftershave.

No, it couldn't be!
I knelt on the floor
Was it on the piano keys perhaps
Just a hint of you left behind.

No, not that.
It was your presence
Reminding me that you were there
Encouraging me to play, despite the tears
Knowing as you always did,
That music would soothe my soul.

✦

The Anniversary

That day
You know the one.
The one where you left me
Standing in that room
Alone

It comes around each year
At first I dreaded it
How could I bear to go through it
The images so clear in my mind
The pain resurrecting

I chose stillness,
To be alone
With my thoughts and tears,
To feel the depth of your absence
So completely
It hurt

But with each year since
I've chosen to celebrate you
To talk about your amazing life
Your music
You, all of you

I sit, raising a glass or several
Celebrating with a dear friend
The man that was you
And I am at peace now on that day
Finally being able to laugh and remember
All the things that made me love you so much.

✦

The Space Between Us

Now that you've gone.
There is a space between us
Sometimes so far I can't sense you
Yet other times, less
The gap closed as your love
Surrounds me

I wonder where your spirit is
Is it somewhere out there
In the ether?
Do you sense me
As I sense you?

Perhaps the space between us
Is only in my mind
I like to believe
That you are fluid
Able to shape shift
Be everywhere
All at once
And so, be by my side
My companion
Still.

✦

Embracing Life

Life... transient
Unexpected
Gorgeously radiant
And then dark and unforgiving
The daily contrast
Challenging me

And yet now...
There is more light,
The luminescence of the day
Shines on me
Filling my heart with joy
And gratitude

The scent of the flowers
Wafting as I walk past
The chirping of the birds
Singing in my ears

The memories of you
Safely stored in my heart
With me always
As I venture out
To embrace this new life.

✦

Transforming Your Relationship

Ahh, how you loved...
With deep soul connection
An ease of being together
That felt so glorious
You don't want to let it go

Nor should you
For the beauty of love
Is that it doesn't stop
After your loved one has died

You remain
The love remains
And now the transforming of your relationship begins

That bond is still present
Just different,
An invisible tether
Linking you,
A continuation of your relationship
But without the physical

How you may ask?
Perhaps you are not spiritual
Perhaps you think that death is it
And that is ok

But the continuing bond
Can be from talking and sharing about them
About beautiful memories you created together
Photos you look at

You choose how to create
Your transformed relationship

But know this...
In doing so
It'll ease some of the loss and pain
And soothe your broken heart.

✦

Bearing Witness

There is no denying
The agony of grief
How it wraps its tendrils
Constricting your heart
And your very being

And you push and rail against it
Go away! Leave me alone!
But it doesn't

As you resist
Those tendrils seem to grow stronger
Squeezing any possibility of hope out of you

But if you did the unthinkable
And allowed it to be,
To hurt,
To express the magnanimity of your loss,
You'd feel a loosening

As you bear witness to your pain
To your loss,
Allowing rather than resisting,
Your grief is heard,
Acknowledged,
And no longer
Has to cling so tightly.

✦

Holding Back

There you are
Feet well and truly stuck in the mud of grief
Unable to move forwards
Holding steady where you are
Afraid to even try to move

Fear has wrapped it's black cloak around you
Stopping you from seeing
That there is hope
There is a new life for you

Maybe you feel disloyal
Thinking that moving forwards
Allowing the grief to subside
Means you'll forget your loved one
So instead you feel an obligation
To stay stuck in it

Do you not deserve to live the life you have left?
For staying rooted in your grief
Will not bring your loved one back

Perhaps choosing to live your life
Is in fact
The best way to honour
You loved one

If fear is holding you back dear one,
Then it is time to dip your toes into your grief
And clear a path to your future.

✦

Triggered

I sit holding the hand of another
Keeping him company
Waiting patiently
For him to make his transition

And I'm triggered
To the memories
Of holding my loved one's hand
Day and night
Those years ago

My eyes filling with tears
As I am but a companion
Dulling the loneliness of this part of his journey

And it strikes me
That I'm about to have another grief
The double grief of Alzheimer's
The first...
As my friend disappeared
Slowly over the years

Maybe tonight or tomorrow
The second grief will arrive
He, released from the awfulness
And me?
A twinge of guilt for the the relief
I will feel
As he is freed.

✦

Avalanche

My friend died today.
An avalanche of emotions
Steamrolled over me,
Grief rising
Tears flowing

It was a blessed release
For him,
An escape from the prison of
Alzheimer's

For me it brought
Grief memories to the surface
From my husband's death
And I was shocked

The heaviness set in
Tired through and through
Brain a little off

And I felt a twinge of relief,
Knowing it was for the best
That he was free,
My heart weeping for his loss

Hurtling back
To strong emotions of grief
Triggered by a different loss,
I was caught off balance
And left ...
Reeling in sorrow.

✦

Aimless

It seems I needed a reminder
Of how early grief feels,
And oh how I feel it
Aimless, lethargic,
Unable to focus,
My brain is just not working.
I start something
Unable to finish it,
I tear up when music is played
A hug leaves me sobbing in your arms.
How strange it feels
To be enveloped again
In a loss that stops me in my tracks,
And I wonder,
Will I move through this
Quicker, easier?
Only time will tell.

✦

Spirit to Spirit

My love...
Physically speaking
You are gone

But spiritually
Ah, that is where the relationship
Has transformed

Spirit to Spirit
I whisper to you
Sharing my innermost thoughts
My pain
My suffering

And when I get quiet
Stillness surrounding me,
I think I can hear your whisper back
'I am still with you'

How I want this togetherness
This intimacy
To continue

Gone but not gone
Loved and still loved
Not present, yet present

A divine mystery
Of connectedness
Spirit to spirit
Soul to soul.

✦

Growing Through Grief

Initially I felt like an emaciated flower.
Lifeless, wilted, sorrowful
My petals had turned brown
Falling one by one
Leaving a bare stalk

But as time went on
I started to nurture this plant
Watering it with love
With self-compassion
Seeking help to support it
Feeding it daily with kind words

And slowly but surely, it started to respond
The stalk became firmer and able to stand alone
New buds appeared
With petals unfurling,
Until one day, quite surprisingly
My flower was in full bloom,
Its scent filling the room with fragrance

Growth through grief
Is possible with loving attention
With the tender care…
Of the gardener of your soul.

Embracing Pain, Maintaining Hope

Embracing the pain?
No, never.
I can't.
I need to push it away.
Avoid, Distract.

Dear one...
It is with loving guidance
That I say
You need to be open to this pain,
To embrace it for its message,
To know that there is value in it

The pain of loss
In its brutality
Is an acknowledgement
Of the depth of love you have
For your loved one.
It is right to feel it,
To mourn them
With all your heart

But what of hope?
Yes, that too.
It's there, behind your veil of sorrow
But waiting quietly
For you to allow it in,
A shaft of light
Allowing hope for the future

There is this balancing act
Of pain, of love, and hope
You need to find the courage
To allow yourself to feel,
While holding onto hope
For a better tomorrow.

✦

*Making
Broken
Beautiful*

By The Thickness Of A Sheet Of Paper!

So small are the improvements
Of a grieving heart,
Getting out of bed
A win on many days

Moving your body
Heavy with grief
Off the sofa,
It doesn't want to move
But you do it anyway

Going to the shops
And not crying in the car,
Noticing when someone smiles at you
And smiling back

It is these tiny moments,
These micro wins,
That remind you
That day by day
You are improving...

By the thickness of a sheet of paper.

And before you know it,
You've made a chapter,
A book,
And somewhere along the way
You started to feel
A new life has begun.

✦

Transcend

Disappearing into a shell of fear
You withdraw from life,
From yourself,
Every second seems to be
Suffused with grief

And yet somewhere within,
A seed of strength is germinating
Pushing you to choose between
Hope and discouragement,
To transcend this crisis
And move toward life.

✦

Running Toward Life Not Away

At what point
In this grief journey
Do we pivot,
And start running toward life, not away?

It is a subtle reroute
So slow
That it is almost imperceptible

The dark road
Shaded, twisty
Winding
Becoming a clear path
Light shimmering through the trees

And you find that
Life appears
Welcoming you with open arms
As you are drawn toward it

✦

Tethered

Dear one
I know the pain is great
All consuming
Unbearable

But you need to untether yourself
From the suffering,
It is time
For you to choose life,
Your life,
And let the cord tying you to the past
Weaken and fray

No, not forgetting your loved one,
Never
Nor stopping your love for them

But easing the pull of the past
To make room for your future,
Travelling with grief,
But not being defined by grief

The pull back in time
To a love lost
Is oh so strong,
But letting go of the pain
Is not letting go of your love

Let the tether loosen
And give yourself permission
To move into your future.

✦

Discovering You

Who am I?
You ask
I have lost me
The me I was with you

So dearest one,
It is time
To go within
And meet yourself
Once more

Sit in stillness
Breathe deeply
Enter your heartspace
For it is there
If you listen carefully
That you can be born anew

Deep inside
You are still there,
You always have been
It is just your situation has changed

Now you must encourage
And nurture
The solo you,
Germinate the seed
Of being,
The one who must emerge
As a new flower in bloom

Go within, my love,
Arrive to yourself,
Release the you that is there
Ready to tackle your new reality.

✦

Courage Revealed

Getting out of bed,
Taking one step after the other
Day after day,
Small acts of courage

Looking at photos of your loved one,
Telling stories,
Sharing their life,
Small acts of courage

Sorting their clothes,
Donating and gifting
That which was theirs,
Small acts of courage

Getting out of the house,
Meeting friends,
Going to a movie,
Small acts of courage

And as you day in day out
Perform these small
Almost insignificant actions,
Remember in your grief that this is…
Courage revealed.

✦

The Waves Of Grief Still Come

Do you remember when those grief waves used to arrive?
They'd knock you over, out of the blue
Leaving you sprawling and trying to pick yourself up.

It felt like they'd never stop.
Their unexpected arrival
Would wash over you
Hurting to the core

And as time passed
As you started to come back to life
The waves receded

Oh they still come
When you least expect them
But they are smaller, less ferocious
And you stand your ground.

And as your foundation becomes more solid
Remember…

Allow the waves to come
Feel the grief
And know that you will survive another day…
Even if a little shaken.

✦

Avenue To Your Healing

Sitting in silence,
A precious gift
If you allow it

The heart murmurs
Messages of intuition,
Do you hear them?

Ah, but you are distracted,
Come back dear one,
To the questions of your being

Oh it is so scary
To just be with yourself,
To go within,
To let your heart open,
To go into deep introspection,
To feel the feelings, the grief
You've managed to avoid

Sit in silence dear one,
It can be an avenue to your healing.

✦

Crossing The Threshold,

The struggle to rise,
To shower,
Even to dress,
Is a daily battle
That you do

One step at a time
You do what you must,
Plodding through the day
Slow as treacle
Getting stuck at times
Grief immovable

But you persist,
And as the days go by,
Small things
Become ever so slightly easier,
Movements become more fluid
Energy starts to enter your body

And you realise
That you have crossed the threshold
From surviving,
To thriving

The days seem brighter,
Smiles appear on your face,
Gratitude for what you had
And what you have now
Becomes apparent

You never thought
When you were in the depths of sorrow
That you'd be able to even live
Never mind thrive

But now my love,
You have finally crossed the threshold
Back to life.

✦

The Power Of Hope

At first,
Hope is a distant thing,
Not even considered,
Something not possible
For your mind or heart
To comprehend

But dear one,
There is in this grief journey
An opening for hope,
If you'll allow it

Are you stuck
Thinking of what was,
What is missing?
Are you going over and over
What you wish
Was different?

Do that for a time,
But don't stay there too long,
For hope doesn't lie in the past
It offers you a hand to your future

And there is a future,
It will be different,
You'll be different,
Everything will be different
Without your loved one,
Accepting that
Is a step you must take

Have courage,
Be ready to look ahead
Maybe just a little way,
Turn your eyes
From the past,
Allow them to wander there
Every so often,
But remind them,
Hope is for the future,
Because there is no hope
Of creating a better past.

✦

The Mosaic Of Life

Death, we want to avoid it,
Deny it
Think it only happens to others,
Until one day, it visits us
Stealing away our loved one

And so it is,
Another part of the mosaic of our life,
The final piece in the jigsaw
Completes the picture

Birth brings such joy and hope,
Life itself, ups and downs,
And then that last piece
We know it will arrive,
Not how or when,
Slotting into its spot
Completing the circle
As we knew it would

Why are we so surprised?
Birth and death
They are just parts of
The mosaic of our life.

✦

Illuminating The Colours Of Life After Grief

Living in grey tones
Everything seemed dull
Lifeless
Colourless
Pointless

But slowly the light peeked in
Illuminating the colours of life.
They were there all along
Just hidden behind my cloak of grief,
Behind the blackness of my eyes

Now the iridescence
Shines bright
Everywhere I see dazzling, vivid, colours,
And I realise,
That it is me who has come back to life
The colours have been revealed to me
Life lost has been found.

✦

Kintsugi Your Heart With Love

Your heart shattered into a million pieces
Crushed by the weight of grief

You can't even imagine
Patching it up,
Becoming whole again

And yet...
It can be done,
Piece by little piece
Gently, tenderly, lovingly

The Japanese art of Kintsugi
Is putting broken pieces of pottery back together
With glistening liquid gold,
A beautiful way to restore something damaged

Could you imagine
Using the same principle
To mend your broken heart?
Gently joining each piece
Not with gold, but love

As you do the grief work,
Of learning to come back to love
Despite the pain,
Finding acceptance in where you are now,
You can discover that your heart
Can be whole in it's put together state,
Because despite the obvious fault lines
There is still beauty in its imperfection.

Now it is whole, but different.

✦

The Grief Remains, But You Expand Around It

It is always there
This loss,
How could it not be?
When your loved one is no longer with you

At first, the grief consumed you,
Everything and every moment of life
Reminded you of their absence

You couldn't imagine that it would ever feel better,
Not even a bit.
And yet, as time went by,
Little things started to spark some joy,
You'd find yourself smiling more often
Even laughing out loud.

And then a grief burst might arrive,
Triggered by a scent or sound,
Reminding you once more
That your grief is there,
Under the surface,
But there nevertheless

The grief didn't change
It remained.
But you?
You changed,
You started to live again,
You accepted that grief would be your companion,
Not your master,
And as you allowed yourself to expand
around that core ball of grief,
Life became more bearable, even pleasurable, once more.

✦

A Brighter Tomorrow

I know.
Hope seems so far off
Hope for what?
Well a new life,
One without your loved one,
But not without the memories you created together,
Not without the love that endures,
But one that has new meaning, purpose and joy

Can there be hope for that?
There can,
If you'll allow it,
If you sit in the grief long enough
For it to start moving through you.
If you choose, yes choose,
That you want to live the life you have left

There is hope for a brighter tomorrow,
For love, and joy
For meaning and purpose.
But you have to decide to be open to it,
And when you are ready
Invite it in,
Let it engulf your heart
Give yourself permission
To heal.

✦

Dear Grief...

Dear grief
You spoke to me before
About listening to your message

I resisted,
Covering my ears
Closing down my heart
I didn't want to hear it

But you persisted
Until I finally surrendered
And was able to absorb what you were saying

I realise now
That my sorrow, my heartache is natural,
If you've loved and lost...
You'll grieve

I didn't understand
That I must feel you
To heal you
That I must allow and acknowledge
So that my broken heart
Can mend

Oh grief,
You've been so painful,
So insistent,
And yet now,
Now that I've listened,
I find you quietening,
Softening,
And you are bearable

You say you'll travel with me
On my journey of life,
Ever present
There to remind me not of the loss,
But of the love that I had...

And through you,
I'll be brought to a place of gratitude, and hope, and finally...
To peace.

✦

The Choice You Make

Oh this grief
This pain
How can I live with it?

Life, my life, so changed
Not the same
Without you

And yet...
I have a life to live
Maybe many years
And so I need to choose
To live it

Ah, but this is so hard,
I can't, I can't go on without you
But, yes, dear one
You can
I promise you

Make the choice to live your life
Choose to honour your loved one
By embracing the life you have left.

✦

Don't Stop Living Because I Died

Dear one,
Can you hear me?

I see you suffering,
Heart breaking, tears flowing

I hear you cry out...
'What's the point?'

I watch as you curl into a foetal position
Not wanting to live

But my love...
It was me who died...
Not you

You are still blessed
With a life to live,
With the light streaming through the window
The stars twinkling at night

You see the daffodils bud
And the roses bloom
And feel the warmth of the sun on your face

Oh how I hope,
That you don't stop living because I died.

✦

Opening To Possibilities As You Move Through Grief

What?
Are you kidding?
Possibilities?

Well yes, actually I'm serious.
Grief affects us all differently
It changes your life,
Changes you,
And we are all touched by it at some time

What I found
As I exited that first year of awfulness,
Was that I had a choice to make.
How was I going to live
The next stage of my life?

And for me,
The choice became,
Do I stay stuck in this grief
Allowing it to consume my whole life?
Or
Can I find a way to start moving through it?

Hard to think of opportunities as you grieve,
Hard to believe anything good could be available to you,
Hard to believe you could feel anything but pain

But as I learned to open my heart,
As I looked for the small daily blessings
New opportunities started to make themselves known

The heaviness of grief
Should be felt,
Should be processed,
And as it softens
May I suggest...
That you are open to unexpected opportunities
Allowing you to create meaning and joy in your life once more.

✦

A New Life Unfolding

A few years have now passed
The grief softened with time,
And a new life unfolds,
A new me discovered

It was unimaginable
That life would go on
Without you,
But it did
Day by day,
Year by year,
It didn't stop for my grief

And as time passed,
I survived
Learning how to live again,
Figuring out how to journey without you,
Allowing the unfolding
Of the new me
Of my new life.

✦

The Woman I've Become

I feel like I've been brought to the new me
Kicking and screaming,
I didn't want to change,
I was happy being me...

Until I wasn't,
Until I didn't know me,
Until I knew that things were different,
No you,
Different me

And so it was,
I was dropped into a new reality,
One that was unfamiliar,
Scary,
Strange

And the only way to survive?
Was to adapt
And that was tough.
Everything at odds
With what life was,
Major readjustments needed

So it began,
The steady reinvention
Of me,
And despite the uphill battle,
A new me emerged

I like the woman I've become,
Stronger, more focused,
And able to carry her love and grief
Together
As she chooses life.

✦

Cracked Open

Loving so deeply,
Grieving so long,
I never thought I'd feel again

I was so dead inside
A hollow shell
Unknown to myself
Without you

And then it happened
When I least expected it
And my heart was cracked open

Was this joy I felt?
A switch had been flicked,
And I felt alive once more

The contrast of emptiness to aliveness,
Of numbness to joy,
Was exquisite.
My broken heart was
Overflowing with love,
And my whole being
Was radiant

I hadn't realised
That all my feelings had been flattened
On this journey of loss,
Grief pushed down,
Joy extinguished,
And I,
Living in the grayscale of life

Dear ones...
Let your heart remain just a little open,
For you never know when
Love and joy might
Decide to visit you.

✦

Acknowledgements

I'd like to start by thanking my dear friend Wendy Plowman for her loving support after Brian's death and for reading my poems and giving me advice on edits and the book cover design. She has been my anchor for the last 5 years, and I can't even begin to express how grateful I am for her.

Thank you to Gail Carroll-Maloney, who has journeyed with me through my grief and I with hers, for all the publicity help she has given to promote this book.

I'd like to thank my sister Nicky Luckett for her support after Brian's death. Knowing what it was like to lose her own husband Paul, she was able to understand and let me be vulnerable and cry without feeling self-conscious.

Thank you to my dear friend Julie Brunswick, whose support through love, life and loss has been unwavering.

Thank you to my beautiful friend Caroline Gibson for keeping me inspired and positive, and encouraging me to publish my poems. Your joyous presence fills my heart and I am so very grateful for you.

Thank you to my old friend Mike Applewhaite for reminding me that I had the creative juice to write and love life again. From one old soul to another, I'm eternally in your debt for this precious gift.

And finally to my late husband Brian Browne. Discovering something new through grief was not what I'd expected, yet here I am writing poetry, all because I lost you. Thank you sweetie pie, you live on in my heart forever.

What Others Have Said About Working With Carol

Here are some words from people I've had the privilege of supporting in their grief.

"There is only one way to get through the grief process... walk right through that fire. Having Carol guide me through the fire gave me support, guidance, and perspective. The skills I learned from her helped me in a million little moments, and people around me could see I was truly dealing with whatever came my way."
— *Patty S.*

"Carol helped me find peace after my dad's death and guided me to release grief I had carried since my younger years. I now feel safe and strong inside, and this is having a positive impact on all aspects of my life."
— *Sarah*

"From our very first call I felt safe with Carol. The tools she has provided me, easy meditations, breathing exercises, written material and mindfulness exercises, have helped immensely in taking tiny steps forward in my darkest moments of grief. I now know that grief will not go away, but it will shift, lighten and I am going to be OK. I highly recommend Carol to guide you through your grief journey."
— *Cheryl G.*

"Talking with Carol allowed me to unpack my feelings around loss. She is relatable and compassionate, and I left our session feeling empowered and full of compassion for others and myself. I felt more like my true self. It's about reframing your thoughts and seeing things differently that can be so healing. Thanks, Carol."
— *Susan T.*

Also by Carol Banens

Alongside this poetry, I have created the *Short Grief Series*. These are short, easy-to-read books written for grievers who want clear, compassionate guidance without feeling overwhelmed. Each book is designed to be practical and digestible, offering the information and support you need to manage the many challenges of grief.

- *Grief Unmasked:*
  The 10 Most Common Myths and Misconceptions

- *Self-Care During Grief:*
  10 Essential Practices

- *Supporting Others In Grief:*
  10 Practical Ways to Help When 'Call Me' isn't Enough

- *Grieving Through the Holidays:*
  10 Practical Tips to Help You Cope

I hope these books, together with this poetry, support you in navigating grief with compassion and courage.

About the Author

Carol Banens is a certified grief educator, grief coach, speaker, and author. After losing her husband Brian to lung cancer, she experienced firsthand the messy and unpredictable nature of grief. Four years later, poetry began to pour out of her, unleashing an unexpected creativity that became part of her healing.

Kintsugi Your Heart: The Art of Living With Grief is her first book, a collection of poems written from the depths of loss and the beginnings of hope. She is also the author of the *Short Grief Series*, concise and compassionate guides that are easy to read and digest for grievers who need practical support. The series includes *Grief Unmasked: 10 Common Grief Myths and Misconceptions*, *Self-Care During Grief: 10 Essential Practices*, *Supporting the Griever: 10 Things to Avoid and What to Do Instead*, and *Grieving Through the Holidays: 10 Practical Tips to Help You Cope*.

When she is not writing or working with clients, Carol enjoys playing the piano, exploring her love of creative writing, and spending time with her two adult children.

A Note from the Author

Thank you for reading *Kintsugi Your Heart*. I know how tender it can feel to face grief, and I hope these poems have offered comfort or connection in some way.

If you have read this book, or any of my others, would you consider leaving an honest star rating and short review on Amazon? It does not need to be long. Even a few words can make a real difference.

Reviews not only mean a lot to me, they also help other grieving people discover these books when they need them most.

You can visit my Amazon Author Page here: https://www.amazon.com/stores/Carol-Banens/author/B0CCW5BDYK

(If you are reading the paperback, simply type this into your browser. In the ebook version, you can just click the link.)

With gratitude,
Carol

Free Resources to Support You On Your Grief Journey

If you would like more support as you navigate your grief, here are a few free resources I have created for you:

- *The Grief Café* — A free monthly online gathering where you can share your story and connect with others who understand. www.carolbanens.com

- *Ease Your Grief Burst Meditation* — A free guided meditation to help when waves of grief feel overwhelming. Download at www.carolbanens.com/griefburst-download

- *10 Coping Tips to Support You Through Grief* — Simple, compassionate tips you can put into practice right away. Download at www.carolbanens.com/10-coping-tips

SCAN
TO DOWNLOAD
YOUR FREE
'TAKING REFUGE'
MEDITATION HERE

www.carolbanens.com

www.ingramcontent.com/pod-product-compliance
Ingram Content Group UK Ltd.
Pitfield, Milton Keynes, MK11 3LW, UK
UKHW042004230426
12048UKWH00009B/545